GOLD'S GYM GUIDE TO FITNESS

FIND BALANCE WITH YOGA AND PILATES

Enslow Publishing
101 W. 23rd Street
Suite 240
New York, NY 10011
USA
enslow.com

THE EXPERTS AT GOLD'S GYM

This edition published in 2019 by Enslow Publishing, LLC.
101 W. 23rd Street, Suite 240, New York, NY 10011

Cataloging-in-Publication Data

Names: The experts at Gold's Gym.
Title: Find the balance with yoga and pilates / The experts at Gold's Gym.
Description: New York : Enslow Publishing, 2019.
| Series: Gold's Gym guide to fitness | Includes glossary and index.
Identifiers: ISBN 9781978506879 (pbk.) | ISBN 9781978506589 (library bound)
| ISBN 9781978506886 (6-pack)
Subjects: LCSH: Yoga—Juvenile literature. | Pilates method—Juvenile literature.
| Physical fitness—Juvenile literature. | Exercise—Juvenile literature.
Classification: LCC RJ133.7 O949 2019 | DDC 613.7—dc23

Printed in the United States of America

To Our Readers: We have done our best to make sure all website addresses in this book were active and appropriate when we went to press. However, the author and the publisher have no control over and assume no liability for the material available on those websites or on any websites they may link to. Any comments or suggestions can be sent by e-mail to customerservice@enslow.com.

Photo credits: All Gold's Glow Photography courtesy of Gold's Gym, with the following exceptions: Jonathan Conklin Photography (p. 11, 16 top); Signorelli, LLC (p. 24 bottom).

All other photos courtesy of Shutterstock.com: Andresr (p. 38–39); Daxiao Productions (p. 41); Marc Dietrich (p. 36 below); Ralph R. Ectinaw (p. 30); f9photos (p. 29); Jack Frog (p. 26); Sebastian Gauert (p. 17 bottom); holbox (p. 31); Izf (p. 36); Blazej Lyjak (p. 14 bottom); michaeljung (p. 8 top); Microgen (p. 20 top); Tyler Olson (p. 20 bottom); Orange Line Media (p. 12); Patrick Photo (p. 25 bottom); Photographee.eu (p. 21 top); Pikoso.kz (p. 22 box); racorn (p. 8 bottom); sharptoyou (p. 35); Syda Productions (p. 18, 33 bottom); Lee Torrens (p. 9); vasanty (p. 24 top); wavebreakmedia (p. 15 bottom, 19 bottom, 25 top).

All exercise instructional illustrations by Remie Geoffroi.

All anatomical illustrations by design36/Shutterstock.com.

All other illustrations courtesy of Shutterstock.com: Icon Craft Studio icon in upper right corner headings.

CONTENTS

INTRODUCTION
A TRADITION OF STRENGTH

In 1965, fitness enthusiast Joe Gold took the knowledge and expertise he'd gained while working out at the world-famous Muscle Beach and opened his first gym in Venice, California.

This first Gold's Gym featured homemade equipment and a can-do spirit that made it an instant hit with local bodybuilders. In 1977, the gym gained international renown when it was featured in the movie *Pumping Iron,* starring Lou Ferrigno and a Gold's Gym regular by the name of Arnold Schwarzenegger.

Joe Gold's passion for fitness was the driving force behind that original location's success. Today, that same passion can be found in the staff, trainers, and members at over 700 clubs across America and around the world in countries including Japan, Australia, Venezuela, Russia, India, the Philippines, and beyond.

Gold's Gym remains the go-to gym for celebrities and professional athletes—and anyone looking to get into the best shape of their life. No matter what your fitness goals may be, you'll find the latest and best equipment, classes, and services to suit your needs, whether that means getting ready for a beach vacation or looking to make major life changes.

But more importantly, at Gold's Gym you'll find a welcoming and supportive community. For more than 50 years, Gold's Gym has been showing people that strength comes in many forms. Joe Gold realized that everybody has a unique journey to achieving their health and fitness goals. Today, we're still dedicated to helping you set and attain those goals, in the gym and throughout your life.

Increasing your flexibility—with stretching exercises, massage, and various exercise classes—becomes another piece of the fitness puzzle that can keep you moving comfortably and exercising robustly throughout your life.

WORK OUT ON THE GO

In order to extend your fitness plan, consider adding workouts to areas of your life beyond the gym. While on vacation or a business trip, seek out the hotel fitness room or swimming pool—or turn your room into a mini gym with a toolkit of lightweight workout aids. Perform stretches or resistance training exercises while at the office or even while commuting to and from work. And don't forget to involve important people in your life, like friends and family members. Kids, especially, can benefit from the discipline and structure of regular exercise sessions.

UNDERSTAND INJURIES

Injuries to muscles or joints are always potential threats for an exercise regimen, especially if you're broadening your scope or increasing your lifting load. Learn to recognize minor injuries (and the difference between treating them with heat versus ice packs) and how to determine if a visit to a doctor is in order. Understand how to apply the stretching and limbering techniques that will allow you to recuperate swiftly and resume your workouts.

STAY FIT AT ANY STAGE OF LIFE

No matter where you are in life you should always be able to get a workout. Pregnancy shouldn't derail fitness goals. There are effective, gentle ways to help women prepare for the birthing process and equally effective ways to return to pre-baby shape. Seniors, perhaps more than anyone, benefit from keeping active and flexible. Studies have shown that arthritis pain and stiffness can be reduced through exercises or classes, like yoga, that focus on mobility.

MAKE IT A FITNESS LIFESTYLE

Getting fit is not just about reaching a strength or endurance goal or a desired weight; it's also about retaining that conditioned physique and adhering to the lifestyle changes you made. You will find that mental attitude is just as critical for maintaining fitness as it is for achieving it. Yet, once you find yourself looking and feeling strong and confident, those gains will reinforce your will to stick to your fitness plan for years to come.

STAY LOOSE

Limberness, is the ability to move flexibly—to stretch up, down, or sideways, and bend, squat, and twist—with fluid ease. In fitness terms, flexibility means more than simply being able to touch your toes. Flexibility helps prevent injury during exercise, loosens you up so that your muscles and joints can move through their full range of motion during weight work, such as lifts and squats, and it improves your overall posture. This latter benefit is especially important to the large portion of the workforce that hunches over a computer keyboard all day.

Flexibility also means an increased blood flow to your muscles, and it can even help ward off occasional or chronic back pain. Staying active and stretching are both simple ways to improve your flexibility and prevent the loss of mobility that often affects people as they age.

Ask the EXPERT

WHEN DO I STRETCH?

One thing trainers generally agree on is that stretching, which offers so many benefits to the body, needs to be included in a fitness plan. But its placement, duration, type, and intensity are often debated, and different trainers have differing answers. You can stretch both during and after strength exercises, but beforehand, the muscles must be first thawed out and thoroughly warm prior to stretching. Although some general light stretching when "cold" probably won't result in a muscle tear, it is best to ease into stretching when the body is warm and properly up to speed. It is good to stretch the working muscles between your sets to keep them warm and pliable.

STRETCH IT OUT

What most people traditionally think of stretching is holding your body in an extended posture for a few seconds, like thrusting your arms over your head as you yawn. There are three basic types of stretches: static, dynamic, and ballistic. Other advanced techniques that combine passive and active stretching are often employed by physical therapists.

STATIC STRETCHING Static stretching consists of holding a joint in a stretched position for a designated length of time, typically 10 to 30 seconds. This stretch allows a muscle to slowly adapt to a new range of motion; it is considered passive because the muscle remains relaxed the entire time.

DYNAMIC STRETCHING Dynamic stretching utilizes an increased range of motion, through the use of body-weight exercises such as squats or lunges. As the body moves in multiple planes of motion, the muscles both contract and relax. These active stretches help prepare the muscles for a hard training session, such as running or cycling.

BALLISTIC STRETCHING Ballistic stretching forces the body into a deeper stretch by using powerful movements—such as bobbing up and down to touch the toes. Ballistic stretches increase risk of injury and don't improve flexibility, and, in some cases, they actually cause muscles to tighten up.

STAY STILL

An isometric, or static, contraction is a type of stretch that creates tension in a muscle without changing its length. Stretching out your leg on a chair is a passive stretch. If you contract your hamstrings—by trying to bend your knee by putting pressure on your heel, for example—the stretch becomes isometric. This, in turn, increases the range of motion. You can use the floor, a wall, a chair or a partner to create the resistance needed to achieve the static contraction of an isometric stretch.

Isometrics also allow you to increase your strength in stretched positions so that, during a lunge for instance, your legs do not slide out of control. Muscle strength is increased during isometrics because, in a stretched muscle, not all fibers will elongate, whereas when a contraction occurs in a stretched muscle, more of those resting fibers will react—and those already stretched will elongate to an even greater extent.

Typically, for most general fitness goals and weight loss, it is best to include as many muscles of the body as possible in an exercise session to get the most out of your isometric work and provide a full-body effect. Isometrics are not recommended for those under 18, nor are they advised for warm-ups—they are considered too intense.

INCREASE YOUR FLEXIBILITY

Increased flexibility can enhance performance during aerobic training and muscular conditioning, as well as in sports. As such, it should be an ongoing goal of your fitness plan. Stretching not only benefits muscles and joints, it also prepares you for strenuous exercise. Massage and relaxation therapy can help you ease those knots of tension and loosen up.

START WITH DYNAMIC WARM-UPS Begin your cardio workout with dynamic stretches such as squats, lunges, side lunges, push-ups, and jumping jacks. Perform at least two of these—three sets of 20 reps will get your body ready for a serious workout.

END WITH STATIC STRETCHING Post-workout, try long-duration static stretches to lengthen muscles made tight by weight lifting. Your chest, lats, or hip flexors may also need work due to daily stresses on posture.

APPLY FULL RANGE OF MOTION Partial range-of-motion workouts may increase strength, but using a full range of motion will boost your limberness. Full-depth squats, for instance, improve hip flexibility. When lifting, first perform full-range exercises with lighter weights.

UTILIZE MASSAGE This hands-on approach boosts flexibility by breaking up the knots in muscles and tissues that restrict motion. Applying foam rollers pre-workout will prepare you for exercise; afterwards, they can flush away waste products. Focus on the key players: calves, quads, upper back, and lats. Visiting a massage therapist several times a month can also ensures that you get muscular relief.

TAKE TIME TO RELAX Nothing tightens up the body like stress, which can occur when the mental pressures of home and work combine with the physical demands of the gym. To counteract stress, seek out a relaxing activity like walking, light yoga,or a recreational dance class a few times a week to help your mind—and joints—open up.

BE AWARE The issue of whether or not you should stretch before you exercise is still disputed. Based on various studies, some trainers advise stretching beforehand, while others say to avoid it. For instance, weight lifters may find themselves weakened by warm-up stretches. The best course is to discuss when and how to stretch with your trainer, someone who understands your specific fitness requirements.

LIMBER UP

Begin your day with this quick full-body stretch routine. When performing these moves, focus on isolating the targeted muscles and moving with control. The more you practice, the easier it will become for you to move with fluid grace. Be sure to hold each stretch for 30 seconds, using whatever form of timekeeping that works best for you.

A LYING-DOWN PRETZEL STRETCH Lie on your back, with both legs elongated and parallel and your arms extended away from your torso, palms facing up. Bend your right leg and place the sole of your foot on the floor. Lift your butt off the floor, tilting your torso slightly to your left, and cross your right leg over to your left side, with your knee bent at a right angle. Hold, and then return to the starting position. Repeat on the other side.

B UNILATERAL LEG RAISE Place your hands on your right hamstring just below your knee, and then extend your right leg toward the ceiling, pointing your toes. Hold, and then lower your leg. Repeat on the other side.

C SIDE-LYING RIB STRETCH Lie on your right side with your legs together and extended. Place both palms on the floor, your right arm supporting you and your left arm positioned in front of your body. Your upper body should be slightly lifted. Bend your left leg, and rest your foot just in front of your right thigh, knee pointing up toward the ceiling. Keeping your legs in place, press down with your hands as you raise your body upward, feeling a stretch around your right rib cage.

D GOOD MORNING STRETCH Stand tall with your legs and feet parallel, shoulder-width apart. Keep your knees soft, and tuck your pelvis slightly forward. Reach your arms fully up toward the ceiling, keeping them long and parallel with your body. Focus your energy on the middle of your palms, which should be facing inward. Turn your gaze upward as you stretch. You should feel a stretch from your toes to the tips of your fingers.

E FORWARD LUNGE WITH TWIST Stand with your feet together, hands on your hips. Lunge forward on the right leg, focusing on a downward movement of your hips, until your thigh is parallel with the floor. Bend forward to place your hands on the floor on either side of your right foot. Balance your weight on your left hand, and carefully and slowly guide your right arm up toward the ceiling, twisting your torso. Return to the starting position, and repeat on the other side.

F SIDE LUNGE STRETCH Stand with your feet wide, toes facing outward. Bend your knees and hips to slowly lower into a sumo squat. Once you feel the stretch in your glutes and hamstrings, drop your hands onto the floor in front of you, transferring some of your weight onto your arms. Staying as low as possible, slowly shift your body to the right, bending your right knee while extending and straightening your left leg. Rise to the sumo squat position, and then stretch to the other side.

EXERCISE	TIME/SETS/REST	TARGET
LYING-DOWN PRETZEL STRETCH	Hold for 30 seconds for two sets on each side with a 10-second rest between sets.	Rotator muscles, chest, and glutes
UNILATERAL LEG RAISE	Hold for 30 seconds for two sets on each side with a 10-second rest between sets.	Lower back, groin, glutes, and hamstrings
SIDE-LYING RIB STRETCH	Hold for 30 seconds for two sets on each side with a 10-second rest between sets.	Rib cage, lower back, obliques, and outer thighs
GOOD MORNING STRETCH	Hold for 30 seconds for two sets with a 10-second rest between sets.	Back, neck, abs, obliques, palms, forearms, and upper arms
FORWARD LUNGE WITH TWIST	Hold for 5 seconds for four sets on each side with a 10-second rest between sets.	Quads, glutes, hip adductors, hamstrings, obliques, rib cage, shoulders, and chest
SIDE LUNGE STRETCH	Hold for 5 seconds for four sets on each side with a 10-second rest between sets.	Hip adductors, hip flexors, hamstrings, inner thighs, and glutes

BREATHE DEEP Don't forget to breathe as you stretch: proper breathing helps your body to relax, and it increases blood flow to your internal organs. Exhale as you move into the stretch, and then once you are in the stretch, inhale deeply. To relax the muscles in the back of your neck and your diaphragm (which lets oxygen in to feed your muscles), relax your jaw, letting your mouth hang just slightly open.

STRETCH WITH A BUDDY

You don't need any equipment to stretch effectively, however, working with another person offering resistance can enhance your routine. Perks include a greater degree of flexibility and an increased range of motion. Some Olympic athletes even use partner stretches to get in shape for their events. As with any shared fitness activity, your buddy will help keep you accountable—so you meet up at the agreed times.

Among the many ways to stretch with a partner is PNF, or proprioceptive neuromuscular facilitation. One version of PNF is contract-relax stretching, by which you contract a muscle isometrically against resistance provided by your partner. You rest for several seconds, and then your partner helps you move that same muscle into a passive stretch. The typical duration is six reps before you switch places. Another version, known as hold-relax stretching, calls for a passive stretch followed by an isometric one. Any form of PNF can purportedly increase limberness even more than regular stretching.

When it's your turn to be the helper, you will use your body to provide leverage. To lower the risk of injury, use the major muscles of your legs and trunk to resist your partner's movements. Avoid unnecessary twisting or bending, and stop if you feel pain in either role.

CHOOSE YOUR PARTNER

If you are interested in partner stretches, it's wise to first work out with a personal trainer or physical therapist familiar with the movements. Once you have mastered the various techniques, try them out with a gym buddy, friend, or family member. There is a theory in the fitness community that romantic couples who stretch together can increase their bond—forging a strong sense of connection and trust. To amplify this effect, stretches that involve facing each other should also include lots of held eye contact. Imagine an exercise regimen that not only gets you in shape, but also improves your relationship!

Here are some tips to follow when working with a partner, to focus on safely and properly helping each other stretch.

DO Let the desire to keep up with your partner motivate you to work past performance plateaus.

DON'T Avoid continuing with any stretches in either role if you begin to feel pain. Stretching should never hurt.

DO Combine social time with fitness by stretching with a friend with whom you rarely spend one-on-one time.

DON'T If your partner corrects your form, don't be offended. Make safety a priority while giving proper leverage and control.

DO IT À DEUX

The following quick stretch routine offers you and your partner an introduction to the hold-relax method of PNF stretching. For each of these exercises, the helper should move the stretcher to the point of being in a comfortable yet challenging stretch. The stretcher then isometrically contracts those targeted muscles by gently pushing against the force of the helper's movement. For example, during this phase of the assisted, unilateral leg raise, as the helper pushes the elevated leg back, the stretcher pushes it forward with the same force so that the leg remains static. After holding this passive stretch for 10 seconds, both helper and stretcher relax before repeating all steps, this time holding the passive portion for 30 seconds.

A ASSISTED UNILATERAL LEG RAISE This stretch targets the hamstrings, calves, and glutes.

HOW Assuming the role of helper, stand to the right, and face the stretcher, while the stretcher lies faceup on the floor. Take hold of the stretcher's right leg as the stretcher lifts it toward the ceiling, positioning yourself so that the lower calf rests comfortably on your right shoulder. Place your other hand on the thigh just above the kneecap. The stretcher then leans in toward you, providing a comfortable stretch and holding this position for 10 seconds before relaxing. Then, while you provide resistance, the stretcher pushes the leg against your shoulder, holding for 6 seconds, and then relaxing. Repeat again, this time holding the stretch for 30 seconds. Perform a second set, and then switch your roles.

B ASSISTED CHEST STRETCH This stretch targets the chest and shoulders.

HOW The stretcher sits on the floor with legs slightly bent, heels together, and hands clasped behind the head. As the helper, stand behind the stretcher with your knees bent and slightly knocked inward, so your knees are at the sides of the stretcher's middle back. Place the inside of your forearms on the inside of the stretcher's upper forearms and inside of the biceps. Pull the stretcher's arms in toward yourself, while providing stability with your knees on the middle back. Hold for 10 seconds, relax, and then repeat, this time with the stretcher pushing against your resistance. Hold for 6 seconds, and then relax. Repeat again, this time holding the stretch for 30 seconds. Repeat for a second set, and then switch your roles.

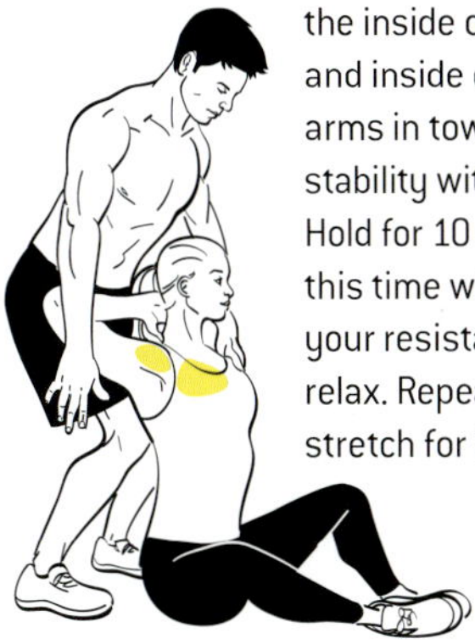

C ASSISTED SEATED FORWARD BEND This stretch targets the hamstrings, lower back, upper back, and calves.

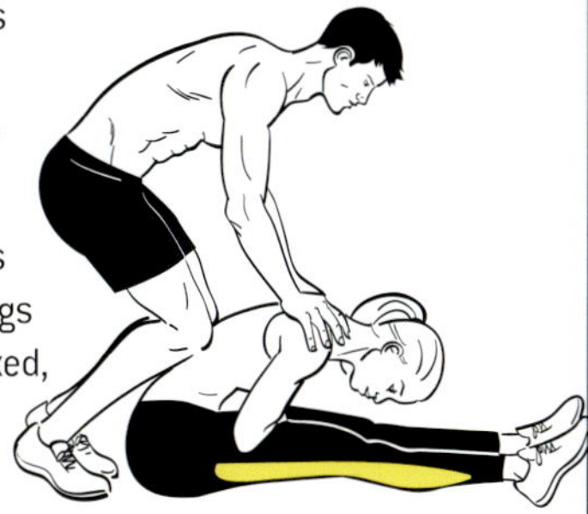

HOW The stretcher sits on the floor with both legs extended, feet in a relaxed, flexed position. The stretcher then relaxes the weight of the upper body over the thighs. As the helper, stand behind the stretcher, and bend your legs so that your shins lightly rest on the stretcher's lower back. Put your palms on the stretcher's shoulder blades. Apply gentle pressure with your hands and your shins to create a comfortable stretch for your partner. Hold the stretch for 20 to 30 seconds. Relax, and repeat for a second set, and then switch your roles.

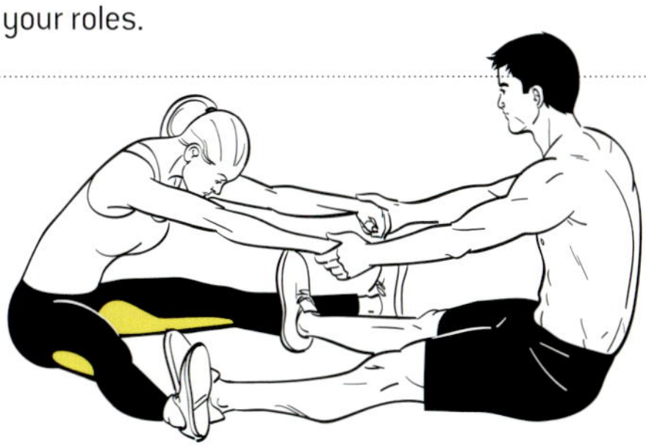

D RUSSIAN SPLIT SWITCH This stretch targets the hamstrings and hip adductors.

HOW Sit upright facing each other with your legs spread as widely as is comfortable, with your feet slightly flexed and legs turned out from the hips so that your toes point upward. The soles of your feet should rest above each other's inner ankles. Reach out, and clasp hands. You then lean back slightly, moving your partner forward. Hold for 20 to 30 seconds. Relax, and repeat for a second set, and then switch roles so that your partner brings you forward.

KNOW YOUR... IT BAND AND TFL

The iliotibial band, usually just called the ITB or IT band, is a thick band of fibrous tissue that runs down the lateral or outside part of the thigh, beginning at the iliac crest (the border of the most prominent bone of the pelvis) and extending to the outer side of the tibia (the shinbone), just below the knee joint. The ITB also attaches to the gluteal muscles and the tensor fascia latae (often called the TFL). The tensor fasciae latae is the muscle on the outside of your hip that moves your leg outward. The ITB functions in coordination with several of the thigh muscles to provide stability to the outside of the knee joint.

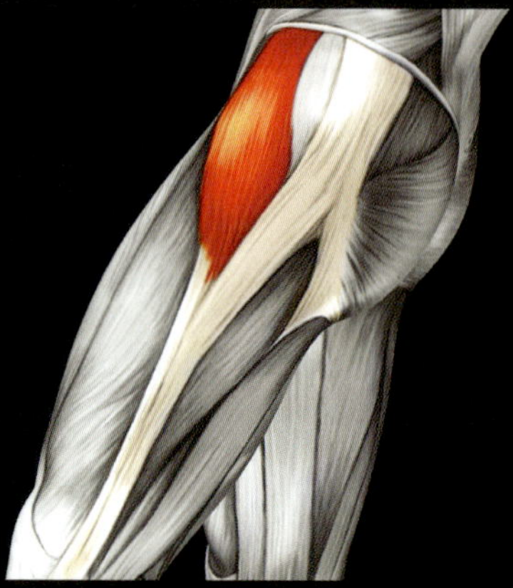

RECOGNIZE THE SIGNS

Many runners, cyclists, hikers, dancers, and other athletes experience a common injury called iliotibial band syndrome, or ITBS. In these activities, the IT band, which helps stabilize the knee, continually rubs over the lower extremity of the femur while it moves from behind the bone to in front of it. This friction, along with the repeated flexion and extension of the knee that all of these activities demand may cause the iliotibial band area to become inflamed, producing hip and knee tightness and pain.

ITBS, one of the leading causes of lateral knee pain in runners, is sometimes caused by physical abnormalities, such as high or low arches, pronation or supination of the foot, bow legs, or uneven leg length. Another culprit could be muscular imbalance—weak hip abductor muscles or uneven left/right stretching of the band, possibly caused by sitting cross-legged. Foam roller massage may be helpful in preventing and relieving the discomfort ITBS produces.

SYMPTOMS Signs of ITBS include a stinging sensation above and outside the knee joint or along the whole band, tightness of the band, or swelling of the tissue where the band rubs over the femur. Most often, when ITBS occurs, an individual will no longer be able to run, but can continue to walk and perform other activities.

DIAGNOSIS Pain may not always be present during activity, but it is usually felt as the foot strikes the ground or as you turn a corner when running, or, especially, as you walk down stairs. Some borderline sufferers choose not to see a doctor, but the pain can intensify over time if not treated.

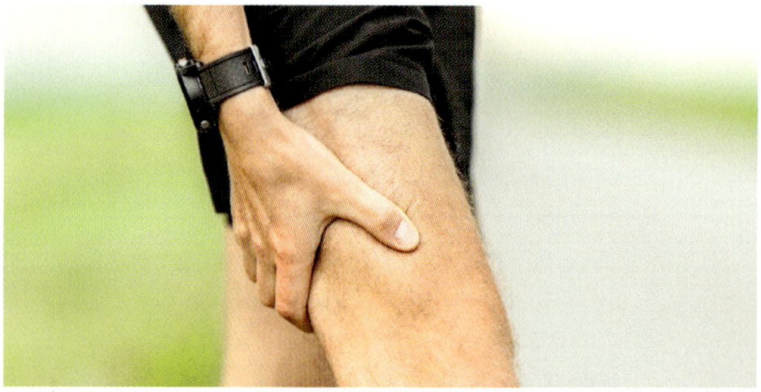

CAUSES ITBS often results from certain training methods—habitually running on a banked track or cambered surface, requiring the downhill leg to bend inward, excessively stretching the band against the femur; not warming up properly; a pounding foot strike; or too much up-and-down hill or stair work. Long-distance running, as well as other athletic pursuits, such as cycling with angled-in toes, hiking long distances, rowing, swimming the breast stroke, and water polo, can sometimes be at fault. Even a change of footgear, perhaps made to address another problem, can cause a flare-up.

TREATMENT Rest, icing, compression, and elevation (RICE) are initially essential for healing. Some form of massage therapy, even self-massage, can also help offer relief. Early treatment is key—research has shown that three days of immobility (through bracing the affected knee) and use of crutches cured a majority of acute ITBS cases. Once you are back on the road, limit the frequency, duration, and intensity of runs, always warm up first, and place an ice pack on your leg afterward. In future, avoid any potentially painful stimuli, like running downhill.

KEEP IT SUPPLE

If you are prone to ITBS, a fitness plan that includes stretching the IT band is the best way to alleviate any inflammation or irritation. Pay careful attention to how long you hold each stretch. For these kind of stretches to be effective, you must remain in the pose for 30 to 60 seconds, and repeat two or three times. To start, try these three stretches, which might help to keep your IT band supple and pain-free.

A CROSSOVER TOE TOUCH Crossing one foot over the other helps to keep the focus of this stretch on the outside of your thigh. Like any toe touch, it will also stretch your back and hamstrings muscles.

HOW Start standing. Cross one leg over the other. Bend at the waist with the goal of touching your hands to your toes.

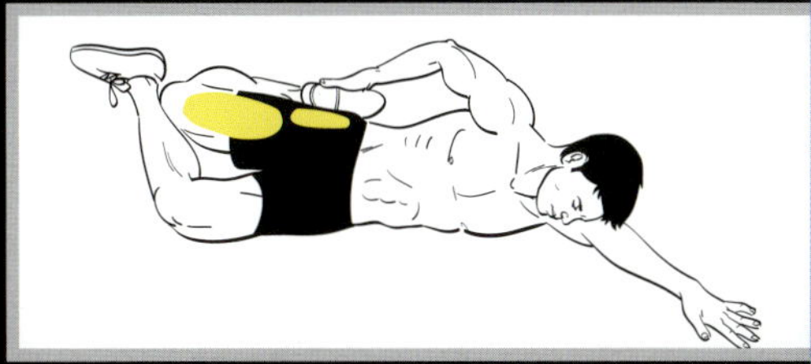

B SIDE-LYING IT BAND STRETCH This stretch can help keep your IT band flexible, while also stretching your quads.

HOW Lie on your side. Kick your top leg back, and grasp your foot. Bend your bottom leg, and tuck the ankle over the knee of your top leg. Repeat on the other side.

C PIGEON STRETCH Try this yoga-inspired seated stretch to target your IT band.

HOW Start in a push-up position. Bend one knee, and move your leg forward until you can rest the outside of your knee and foot on the floor. Gently press down on your hip, while distributing the weight between your hands and your bent leg.

RELEASE THOSE KNOTS

When stretching a muscle with painful knots in it, you only end up stretching the healthy muscle tissue—the knot remains intact. In most cases, massage is needed to relieve these knotted muscles. If you don't have your own masseuse, consider hands-on massage using a ball or foam roller, a process known as self-myofascial release, or SMFR. In this technique, gentle pressure slowly loosens the painful myofascial tissue restrictions that can be caused by injury, inflammation or surgical procedures—and which often do not show up on x-rays or scans. SMFR can reduce the risk of injuries, and it can also help you to achieve long, lean muscles, while improving flexibility, functionality, and athletic performance. Although it's considered a form of alternative medicine, many physical therapists rely on SMFR.

Myofascial therapy administered with a small flexible ball, such as a massage ball or even a tennis ball, may offer the greatest reward for the smallest price. A ball this size can travel with you anywhere—you can even use it for a discreet massage at work or on an airplane. This kind of massage relieves pain and physical stress and helps the body become more limber, as well as easing foot and calf muscle cramps (especially those caused by high heels). Try it on your calves, hamstrings, glutes, quadriceps, and back.

SERVE IT UP

To give yourself a relaxing foot massage, try this form of SMFR using nothing more complicated than a simple and readily available tennis ball. Just sit comfortably on a chair in your bare feet. Place a tennis ball under the arch of one foot, and roll it back and forth, going all the way from the ball of your foot to the heel. Then carefully return it to the arch position. If any areas feel tight or crampy, apply some extra pressure. Continue the process for 60 seconds, rest, and then repeat. Switch feet, and repeat the sequence.

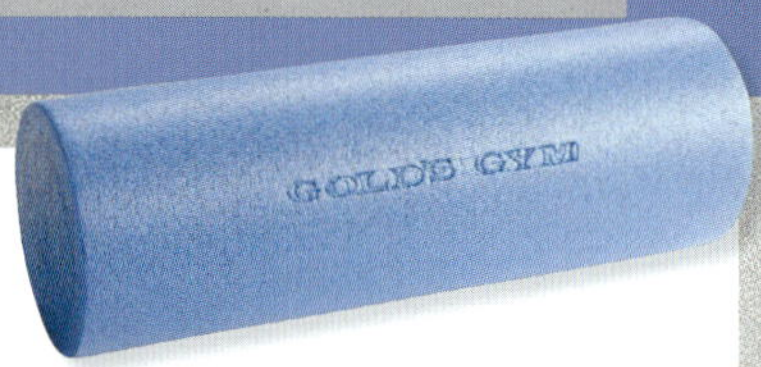

TOOLS of the TRADE

FIND RELEASE WITH A FOAM ROLLER

The tool most often used to apply SMFR is a roller, usually made of dense foam or knobbly rubber and shaped like a bolster pillow. You simply roll your body over the roller, and when you find a tender spot or trigger point, you keep pressure on that area until the pain lessens by half or more. Eventually, you will be able to roll over that spot without pain.

Make sure you control your body weight on the roller to generate the pressure necessary to break up problematic spots. Roll back and forth across any stiff, painful areas for approximately 60 seconds, rest for 10 seconds, and repeat. Maintain a slight contraction in your abdominal muscles to stabilize and protect your core (lower back, pelvis, and hips) during the rolling process. Keep your breathing slow and natural to reduce any tension caused by the discomfort the roller sometimes produces. Be careful not to roll over bony areas, such as elbows or knees. Follow up with stretches that target the muscles you just focused on. Remember, you can treat your specific trigger points before they knot up.

In addition to their therapeutic effectiveness, these foam rollers offer other benefits.

ADAPTABILITY The roller lets you control the amount of pressure placed on the trouble spots.

COST These rollers make a relatively inexpensive fitness tool.

PORTABILITY A small foam roller can travel with you to work or on vacation.

CONVENIENCE You can experience a customized massage any time you wish.

ROLL WITH IT

Practicing self-myofascial release with a foam roller can help you relieve the muscle aches and knots that can develop after rigorous strength workouts or intense cardio sessions. This kind of massage will also aid in the removal of metabolic waste, such as lactic acid, from the muscle. These exercises target four common areas of post-workout soreness: the IT band, calves, hamstrings, and back. Perform foam roller stretches three times a week to prevent stiffness and injury, and feel free to roll over any tense or knotted areas two to three times a day.

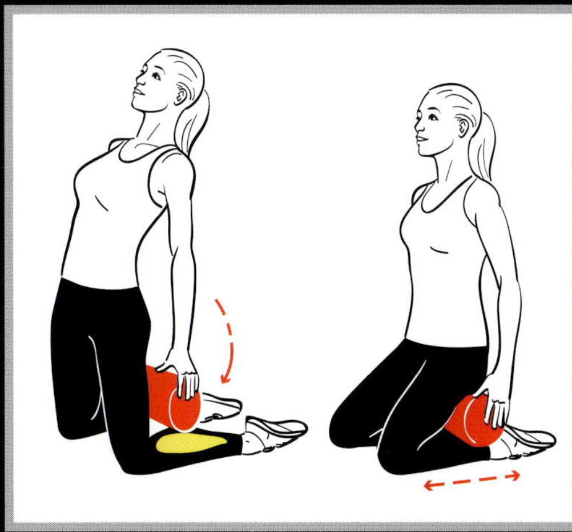

A FOAM ROLLER BACK STRETCH This stretch targets your back muscles, including the lats and erector spinae.

HOW Sit with your knees bent and your feet flat on the floor, shoulder-width apart. Place the roller behind your lower-back region. Lean back carefully onto the roller. Raise your hips slightly off the floor, lifting your butt as you simultaneously take small steps forward, allowing you to begin rolling the foam roller upward on your back with your hands clasped behind your head or in front of you. Pause over uncomfortable areas before rolling back and forth over them until you feel relief. Continue rolling for 60 seconds. Rest, and then repeat.

B FOAM ROLLER CALF AND HAMSTRINGS STRETCH

This exercise targets your gastrocnemius and hamstrings.

HOW Kneel upright, and place the foam roller behind your knees. Carefully rock your pelvis slightly forward, just enough to place the foam roller deep behind your kneecaps. Lower your body weight by sitting gently on the foam roller. As you begin to sit, you will find that the foam roller naturally moves over your calf muscle. Guide the roller with your hands, moving the roller slowly down toward your heels.

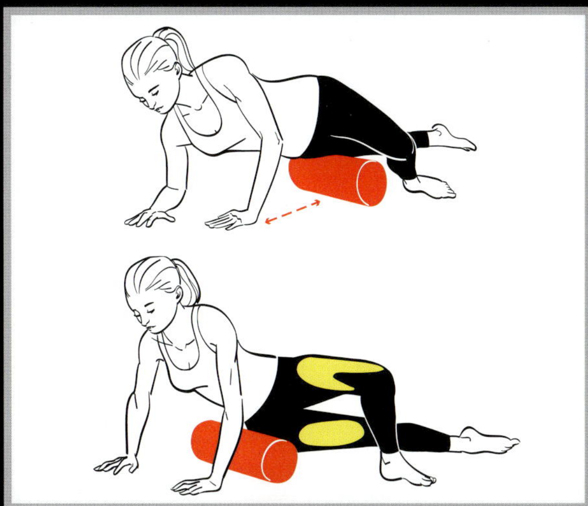

C ITB ROLL This stretch will target your IT band and quads.

HOW Rest your right upper thigh against the roller, bend your left knee up toward your right knee, and then place as much of your foot on the floor as possible. Tilt your body slightly to the right, adjusting your body weight to achieve the desired pressure on your upper thigh, rolling slowly down to just above your knee. Pause over uncomfortable areas before rolling back and forth over them until you feel some relief. Continue rolling for 60 seconds. Rest, and then repeat. Switch sides, and repeat.

COMBINE BALANCE AND COORDINATION

Balance and coordination are two additional components of the fitness equation, as well as major factors in many competitive sports. Balance is the ability to remain upright and stay in control of your movements. Humans use their eyes, ears, and proprioception or "body sense" to help stay balanced. There are two types of balance: static and dynamic—maintaining equilibrium while staying still, and while moving, respectively.

As we age, the ability to balance well can deteriorate—sometimes as early as in our twenties. Retaining a strong sense of balance can help to ensure personal independence as we enter our golden years; statistically, more than a third of adults over 65 will suffer a fall, which is the number one cause of traumatic brain injury in this age group.

Simple actions like walking, climbing stairs, stretching, and resistance training can delay this deterioration, along with exercises that incorporate balance-challenging equipment such as stability balls, BOSU balls, and wobble boards. "Balance exercises speed up your reaction time and improve the brain-to-muscle connection," explains Gold's Gym Fitness Institute trainer Ramona Braganza.

Coordination, the ability to skillfully combine multiple actions, not only requires good balance, but also agility, sharp reflexes, and strength. As you raise the complexity of your workouts and place more demands on yourself physically, these two components become increasingly important. Fortunately, both can be improved through training and practice.

ACHIEVE PROPER ALIGNMENT

A fit athlete is an aligned athlete. This means that your load-bearing joints are in neutral alignment—where they are at their strongest, at the least odds with gravity, and are able to maximize the use of force, allowing you to use the least amount of energy to maintain a specific position and activate the correct muscles during exercise. Neutral alignment also optimizes breathing and the circulation of bodily fluids.

In neutral alignment, your pelvis is angled to create the optimum space between your vertebrae. There are three curves to your spine: the inward arch of the neck, the outward curve of the mid-back region, and the inward arch of the lower-back region. Neutral alignment helps these curves cushion the spine from excess stress or strain. This stance should be effortless, arising from a healthy and balanced musculature. Here are some guidelines for working toward neutral alignment.

STRADDLE THE SCALES Stand with each foot on a different scale: if they show different weights, your balance is off. This could strain your body during workouts, so talk to a trainer or physiotherapist about realigning your posture and spine.

LOCATE YOUR CENTER Nearly all bodily movements radiate from the central "power pack" of strong muscles around the lumbar spine. One way to improve alignment is to locate this "center," and perform movements that generate from this central core: your abdomen, lower back, hips, and buttocks.

STAND TALL Correct posture requires holding your head up, with chin in, and earlobes aligned with the middle of your shoulders, lengthening your neck, and keeping your shoulders back, knees straight, lower back slightly concave, and abs firm.

TOOLS of the TRADE

SAMPLE THE STABILITY BALL

Stability balls, also known as Swiss balls, exercise balls, body balls, fitness balls, and balance balls, are heavy-duty inflatable spheres originally developed to be used by physical therapy patients. They range in size so you can find one that works best for your height.

The stability ball has become a valued tool of the fitness trainer, the sports conditioner, and the physical therapist. Children, adults, and seniors can use these versatile balls to build strength, improve balance and coordination, work core muscles, and raise endurance. Stability balls are often incorporated into Pilates classes, weight training, and abdominal fitness routines, and their low cost and ease of use make them ideal for the home gym. Stability ball workouts can engage multiple muscle systems, especially those of your core, which challenges your whole body to maintain balance throughout an exercise.

FIND YOUR SIZE

It's important to work with a ball suitable to your height. This chart will help you find the right size (note that size labels such as small, medium or large may vary between manufacturers). Look for one that comes with a pump, and fill it until it is firm and not squishy.

YOUR HEIGHT	BALL SIZE	BALL HEIGHT
Up to 4 feet 7 inches (140 cm)	Extra Small	14 inches (35 cm)
4 feet 7 inches to 5 feet (140 to 152 cm)	Small	18 inches (45 cm)
5 feet to 5 feet 6 inches (152 to 168 cm)	Medium	22 inches (55 cm)
5 feet 6 inches to 6 feet 1 inch (168 to 185 cm)	Large	26 inches (65 cm)
6 feet to 6 feet 8 inches (185 to 200 cm)	Extra Large	30 inches (75 cm)
Over 6 feet 8 inches (200 cm)	Extra, Extra Large	33 inches (85 cm)

TRAIN AND GAIN BALANCE

Balance training is sometimes overlooked as a vital element of fitness conditioning. Fortunately, there are plenty of tools on the market that provide the instability needed to improve your sense of balance. Most of them work by constantly shifting resistance, which challenges the body's center of mass, forcing the core to work harder.

Balance tools can also boost upper body strength. Try a push-up on a balance board—a skateboard-shaped deck that uses a single tubular roller as a fulcrum to simulate lateral and radial movements. Grasp the sides of the board to use as your base as you execute a push-up. The trick is keeping the board evenly balanced. Noting which side you tend to lean toward is a good way to check for your dominant side.

Below are a number of other popular balance aids.

XERDISC Stand on one of these or straddle two of these inflatable rubber balance discs to achieve unstable footing.

BALANCE BEAM This trapezoidal foam plank mimics a gymnast's balance beam and provides a wider or narrower surface for toe-to-heel walking.

ROCKER BOARD This seesaw-like board uses a tubular half circle to create one plane of instability.

WOBBLE BOARD The rounded base of a wobble board furnishes multiple planes of instability.

M-BOARD This board, atop a rounded ball, allows a wide range of movement. A support tripod is also available.

AQUA BOARD Perform normal gym exercises while balancing on a board floating in a pool for a great core workout.

TOOLS of the TRADE

FLIP OVER A BOSU® BALL

The BOSU ball is a balance-training device that was invented in 1999 by David Weck. This inflatable rubber hemisphere, with its rigid platform, can be used dome-side up, offering an unstable top surface with a stable base for athletic drills and aerobics. Dome-side down, it provides an unstable base for balance exercises. (The acronym originally meant Both Sides Up, but now refers to Both Side Utilized.) Some studies have indicated that the imbalance the half-ball provides does not significantly affect muscles, while other studies concluded that working on an unstable surface, at minimum, increases activation of the rectus abdominis muscles.

STAND FIRM

It's hard to believe, but starting as early as your twenties, your sense of balance begins to decrease. How rapidly it diminishes depends on your genes and on the natural process of aging. It also depends on how physically active you are and what kinds of activities you perform. The best exercises challenge your sense of balance by incorporating BOSU balls, wobble boards, and Xerdiscs into your leg workout. Incorporating this equipment not only makes for a more challenging routine, but also builds up your agility. Here are four moves to help you stay grounded.

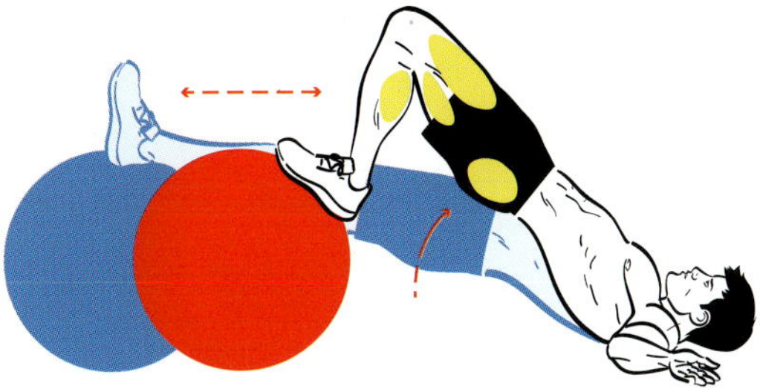

A SINGLE-LEG STABILITY BALL HAMSTRING CURL

This targets your glutes and hamstrings while stabilizing your core. Perform 10 reps.

HOW Lie on your back with your ankles and heels placed on top of a stability ball, toes pointing up. Raise your hips, contract your glutes, and keep your arms out from your sides to stabilize yourself. Roll the ball in toward your hips by rolling from your heels onto the flat part of your feet. Pause momentarily, and then roll the ball back out, making sure to keep your hips elevated.

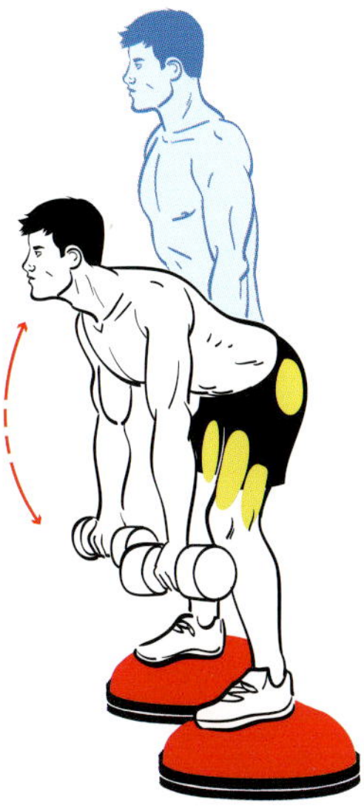

B ROMANIAN DEADLIFT ON XERDISC

Performing this classic strength-building exercise on a Xerdisc targets your glutes, hamstrings, quadriceps, and inner thighs, while also improving your balance. Perform 20 reps.

HOW Place your left foot on one Xerdisc and your right foot on another. Hold a light dumbbell in each hand. Slowly lower from the waist down until your hands are almost to the floor. Then slowly rise back up.

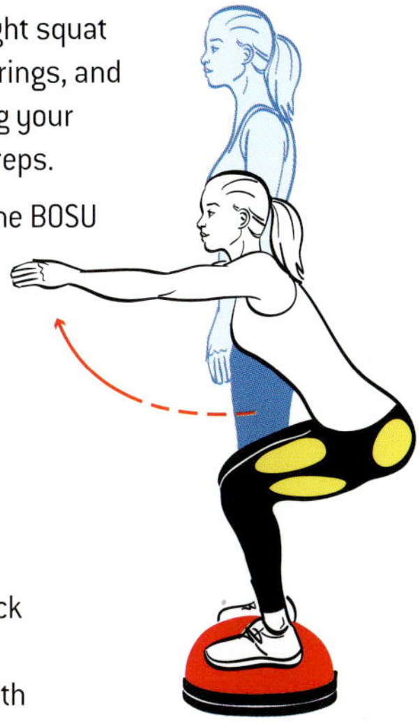

C SQUATS ON A BOSU BALL

This version of a body-weight squat targets your glutes, hamstrings, and quadriceps while improving your balance. Perform 10 to 15 reps.

HOW Begin standing on the BOSU ball, dome side up, with your feet spread as wide as possible and your arms extended forward or clasped in front of you for balance. Descend slowly into a squat until your thighs are parallel to the floor. Pause, then stand back up. To raise the difficulty, attempt the same squat with the dome side down.

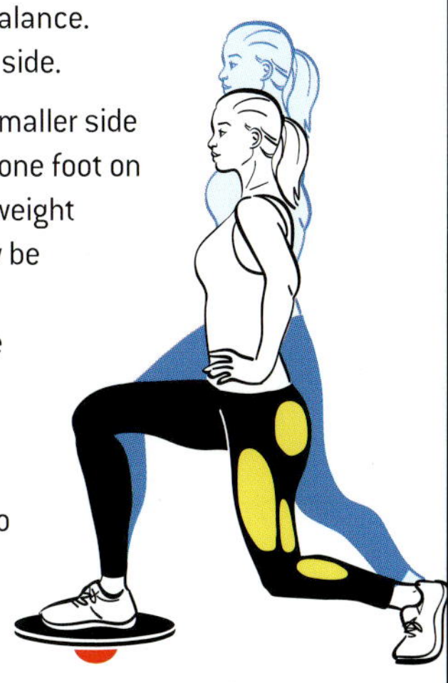

D SINGLE-LEG LUNGE ON A WOBBLE BOARD

Performed on a wobble board, this version of a stationary lunge will target your glutes, quads, hamstrings, and calves while improving balance. Perform 10 reps on each side.

HOW Stand facing the smaller side of a wobble board. Place one foot on the board, shifting your weight to your heel. You will now be in somewhat of a lunge position. Lower and raise your body on the ball of your back foot and the heel of your front foot. Keep the board parallel to the floor. With your foot on the board, make sure that your knee doesn't tracking over your ankle.

OPEN YOUR JOINTS WITH YOGA

The practice of yoga, which developed in India thousands of years ago, was originally meant to educate the body, mind, and spirit. Today, it has become one of the most popular paths to fitness around the world. Yoga promises active flexibility, as it's about full range of motion in your joints. Practicing yoga can help you to increase muscle strength and tone, maintain a more balanced metabolism, lose weight, and improve athletic performance. It can also relieve chronic lower-back pain, soothe inflammation, ease anxiety, boost heart health, and leave you with a euphoric sense of accomplishment.

EASE YOUR CONCERNS

If you want to get started in this peaceful practice, here are suggestions compiled from several yoga pros for overcoming common newbie concerns, along with some additional guidelines.

TOUCH YOUR TOES You don't need to be a circus contortionist to study yoga. In fact, many first-time students are in their 50s or 60s. And if you can't touch your toes or complete certain poses, there are tools or props to aid you.

START WITH THE BASICS Even seasoned athletes who take up yoga need to start with beginner classes. Although yoga poses (called asanas) may look easy, they require a lot of control and attempting advanced movements could result in injury.

RAISE YOUR HAND If you have question, simply ask them during a lull or after class. If the instructor doesn't have an immediate answer, be assured that he or she will find one.

DON'T BE EMBARRASSED Never be afraid of looking silly. Remember, all eyes are on the instructor, not on the new folks who are just figuring things out. Everyone was a beginner at one time. Anyway, in yoga, students help each other: there is no competition.

FIND YOUR STYLE It pays to sample a number of different yoga disciplines, such as hatha, vinyasa, Iyengar, Bikram, kundalini, and ashtanga, and different instructors before making a commitment. Take two classes every week for at least a month.

RELAX AND DECOMPRESS In addition to increased flexibility, relaxation is another great benefit of yoga. Students report that they often leave class feeling like they just went to a spa.

CLEAR THE CLUTTER Yoga helps to clear mental chatter from your mind, by placing you into positions that result in being actively conscious of all your movements, and forcing you to slow down.

FEED BODY AND MIND Yoga's dual nature offers you a better body *and* mind. Many people who initially take yoga to improve their core and reduce body fat stick with it because it also increases confidence, reduces heart rate, and offers a more authentic way of being.

END WITH MINDFUL RELAXATION A yoga session typically ends with its own cool down period—a five-minute full-body relaxing pose called savasana. Some students insist that nothing matters in class as long as you have a great savasana.

PUMP IT UP WITH PIYO®

PiYo, a combination of Pilates and yoga, requires no weights or jumping, however, it can result in a sculpted body and improved flexibility by offering a program of continuous fluid movement. Instead of the sustained poses that are part of a normal yoga class, PiYo speeds things up, introducing dynamic, flowing sequences that burn calories and lengthen and tone your muscles. PiYo classes are not only designed to increase strength and flexibility and improve stability, they also do so with fun, energetic rhythmic choreography that will really get you moving.

TOOLS of the TRADE

ASSEMBLE A YOGA KIT

You will need only a few inexpensive accessories to make the most of your yoga experience.

YOGA MAT Yoga poses are performed on a special "sticky" mat. A yoga mat not only helps define your personal space during class, its tacky surface also creates traction so that you can hold poses, even when you're sweaty. Make sure you use one that is long enough for you to lie down on without your head or feet touching the floor. You can buy a decent mat for the cost of a few barista coffees. For purposes of hygiene, frequently cleanse your mat and other yoga tools with a mild detergent.

YOGA TOWEL "Thirsty" towels made of microfiber work best for absorbing sweat during your session.

YOGA BLOCK A yoga block, which is usually made from compressed foam or cork, can increase your flexibility, allow you to balance more steadily, and provide support so that you can maintain a pose longer and more comfortably. Most yoga studios and classes make these handy tools available to students.

YOGA STRAP These long, narrow straps are used as props to aid movement. They can help you align your posture and ease into poses, especially if you are new to yoga or have tense muscles. They are made of sturdy fabric webbing and have two D-rings on the end so that you can form them into a continuous loop.

YOGA BLANKET Another prop that you'll often see in a yoga studio is a blanket. You can fold or adjust these blankets in any way that you want to support your body in a yoga pose—rolling it up or folding it under your back, legs or neck, for example.

DRESS FOR SUCCESS

The practice of yoga typically requires comfortable, breathable, and somewhat stretchable clothing. One of the beauties of yoga is that you don't need to be an athleisure fashion star to attend classes. On the other hand, there are some items of clothing you might want to avoid.

BOTTOMS Cropped or full-length leggings of a decent weight and in dark colors or yoga pants are fine. Avoid short shorts or loose shorts—these may not be comfortable during some poses. Also, to avoid embarrassment on both sides, ditch those old, worn leggings with tears or holes in the seams.

TOPS Stick with T-shirts, fitted tanks, sports bras, or athletic tops. Avoid too-loose tops or cropped tops that can shift on your body or bunch up during certain forward bends—look instead for long, sleek tops that will stay put and stay comfortable throughout the entirety of your yoga routine.

UNDERWEAR Cotton underwear may become saturated and heavy during a strenuous workout and end up dampening or discoloring your clothing. Spend a little extra for a set of moisture-wicking briefs or boxers.

FOOTWEAR Yoga is traditionally performed with bare feet, but some athletic manufacturers do offer yoga socks, slippers, and shoes with open toes and slip-resistant soles.

INHALE THE FRESH AIR

Nothing is as relaxing as taking an al fresco yoga class in a park or woodland, with the soothing sounds of birds, bees, and the breeze accompanying your asanas. The word *yoga* means "union," and outdoor yoga enables you to feel connected to nature and in harmony with the natural world—all without the artificial "calming" ambience of the indoor class.

Practicing yoga outside can intensify the experience—focusing your awareness, deepening your breathing, and helping to truly practice stillness. It also opens up the sense of smell . . . to pine trees, rivers, oceans, or wildflower meadows. And anything you do outdoors reminds the primitive "hunter-gatherer" part of your brain to become more alert (as a survival tactic) so open-air yoga sessions will likely elevate your energy levels. Conversely, natural settings lower your concentrations of the stress hormone cortisol.

Performing yoga on uneven surfaces, like grass, sand, or woodland trails, can also build up the muscles of your feet, hips, knees, spine, and shoulders.

Check your local gyms or neighborhood website to find where you can participate in outdoor yoga classes.

THINK *about it*

If you feel discomfort or need a break, assume the "time-out" child's pose: kneel on the mat, lower your chest to your thighs, and lower your forehead to the mat. Stretch out your arms or drop them at your sides.

BREATHE DEEP

Yoga fosters both physical well-being and serenity—the positions you assume help to strengthen and elongate your muscles, while your body relaxes through a method of controlled breathing, which is called *pranayama* in Sanskrit. By using these deep, controlled-breathing techniques and by perfecting the various yoga poses, practitioners can refresh both body and spirit.

Breathing can be viewed as a link between the physical and mental aspects of human beings. As such, pranayama, which draws in sustaining oxygen and expels harmful carbon dioxide, should always be incorporated into the asanas that you practice.

Before practicing pranayama while seated, do it lying down in savasana, or corpse pose. Breathe evenly, and focus on filling every part of your lungs with oxygen from the bottom up. First, your diaphragm expands to fill your abdomen, then air fills the middle of your lungs, until it finally reaches the top of your lungs, indicated by the rising of your chest. Both sides of your chest should rise equally. When practicing pranayama while in a seated position, place one hand on your chest and the other on your abdominals to help you observe your breath. Some of the numerous pranayama exercises are listed below.

SAMAVRITTI (SAME ACTION) First, even out any breathing irregularities, and then inhale for four counts, and exhale for four counts. Samavritti calms your mind and creates a sense of balance and stability.

UJJAYI (THE VICTORIOUS BREATH) Maintain samavritti, and then constrict your epiglottis in the back of your throat. Keep your mouth closed, and listen for the *hisssss.* Ujjayi improves concentration.

KUMBHAKA (RETAINING THE BREATH) Begin with ujjayi or samavritti. After four successive breaths, hold your breath for four to eight counts. Then reduce the counts in between held breaths, and increase the number in your inhale. Kumbhaka restores energy.

ANULOMA VILOMA (ALTERNATE NOSTRIL BREATHING) Put your right thumb on the outside of your right nostril, and inhale through your left nostril while keeping your mouth closed. Close your left nostril with your ring finger, and hold momentarily. Lift your thumb, and exhale out of your right nostril. Switch nostrils. Anuloma viloma lowers the heart rate and relieves stress.

SITHALI (THE COOLING BREATH) Curl your tongue, and stick it slightly outside your mouth. Inhale through the divot of your tongue. Retain your breath, close your mouth, and exhale through your nose. Sithali cools the body.

CHILL OUT

Getting fit is not always about the body. It often means changing or adjusting your mental attitude. What better way to approach fitness than with a discipline that teaches you how to focus your thoughts? Yoga meditation consists of "quieting a busy mind," a state you probably often wish for, but rarely achieve. In order to do this, yoga requires you to focus on one specific thing—like your breathing, a small statue, or a candle flame. It does not ask you to maintain a blank mind, only one that refuses to react to the thoughts that do intrude. Ideally, meditation should be practiced at a time of day when you are unlikely to be interrupted and in a place where you can sit comfortably on the floor. Some practitioners find it helps to repeat a resonating mantra, such as *"o-h-m-m-m."*

GET THE RIGHT VIBES

Many of the words used in yoga come from Sanskrit, the classical language of Greater India. It is called a "vibrational" language—merely hearing the words has value, even if their meaning is not understood.

ASANA Seat; yoga posture.

AYURVEDA The ancient Indian science of health.

BUDDHA An enlightened one. "The Buddha" refers to Siddhartha Gautama, an enlightened spiritual teacher who taught in India between the sixth and fourth century BC.

CHAKRA Energy center. The basic system has seven chakras (the root, sacrum, solar plexus, heart, throat, third eye, and crown). Each has its significance and is associated with a color, element, and syllable.

DRISHTI Gazing point used during asana practice.

GURU One who brings us from dark into light; a spiritual mentor.

KARMA Action; the law of karma is the law of cause and effect, based upon the complex web of conditions, individuals and relationships in the universe, not just a simple concept like "steal from someone, and you'll be robbed in return".

MANTRA A repeated sound, syllable, word or phrase; often used in chanting and meditation.

MUDRA A hand gesture; the most common mudras are anjali mudra (pressing palms together at the heart) and gyana mudra (with the index finger and thumb touching).

NAMASTE Greeting commonly translated as "the light within me bows to the light within you"; used at the beginning and end of a yoga class.

OM The original syllable; chanted "o-h-m" at the beginning and/or end of many yoga sessions.

PRANA Life energy; chi; qi.

PRANAYAMA Breath control; breathing exercises.

SAMADHI A state of complete self-actualization; enlightenment.

SAVASANA Corpse pose; final relaxation; typically performed at the end of hatha yoga classes.

SHAKTI Female energy.

SHIVA Male energy; a Hindu deity.

YOGI/YOGINI A male/female practitioner of yoga.

SALUTE THE SUN

This classic yoga flow will energize your body as it stretches and strengthens all your major muscle groups. Known as the sun salutation, or surya namaskar, it is a series of basic poses that appear in most yoga classes. On your first try, hold each of these poses for 10 to 15 seconds, and then flow into the next. Check the chart opposite for the muscle groups worked and the Sanskrit names for the poses, which many yoga instructors will refer to during class.

A MOUNTAIN POSE Stand with both feet touching, back straight, arms pressed against your sides, and your weight evenly distributed on both feet. Flex the muscles in your legs, stomach, and glutes. Bring your hands in front of you in a prayer position

B STANDING BACKBEND From their prayer position, lift your hands until your arms are straight over your head. Lift your chest toward the ceiling, and then bend your shoulders and upper back slowly backward. Stop bending if you experience any pain or discomfort. Hold for two breaths, and then return to mountain pose.

C FORWARD FOLD Bend forward from the hips. Keep your knees straight, and reach your fingertips to the floor. If you can't reach, put your hands on the back of your ankles, or cross your forearms and hold your elbows.

D HIGH LUNGE Bend your knees, then step your left foot back until your right knee forms a right angle. Rest your torso on the front of your thigh, and put your hands on either side of your right foot. Look forward with your neck straight and long.

E PLANK Step your right foot back to meet your left. Hold yourself up in a high push-up stance, your arms perpendicular to the floor, your back straight, and your hips up (not sagging toward the floor).

F HALF-PLANK From plank, lower your torso toward the floor, keeping your elbows tight against your sides until your body is a few inches off the mat. Keep your tailbone firm and your legs active and engaged.

G UPWARD-FACING DOG Lower your body to the floor, then stretch your legs back, pushing the tops of your feet into the floor. Spread your palms on the mat, then push your chest off the mat until your arms are straight. Tilt your head up so that your neck is straight.

H DOWNWARD-FACING DOG Flip from the tops of your toes onto the bottoms, while also pushing your hips up into the air. Your body should form an upside-down V with your palms on the mat and your fingers spread wide. Push your heels down toward the floor, then widen your shoulder blades, and pull them toward your buttocks.

I HIGH LUNGE See D, but step back with your right foot to reverse the movement of the pose.

J FORWARD FOLD See C.

K STANDING BACKBEND See B.

L MOUNTAIN POSE See A.

EXERCISE	TARGET	SANSKRIT NAME
MOUNTAIN POSE	Legs, glutes, and stomach	Tadasana
STANDING BACKBEND	Abdominals, rib cage, arms, chest, and back	Ardha anuvittasana
FORWARD FOLD	Glutes, back, hamstrings, and calves	Uttanasana
HIGH LUNGE	Hip flexors, quads, glutes, and hamstrings	Aekpaadprasarnaasana
PLANK	Abdominals, lower back, chest, neck, shoulders, upper trapezius, biceps, triceps, glutes, thighs, and calves	Kumbhakasana
HALF-PLANK	Abdominals, lower back, chest, neck, shoulders, upper trapezius, biceps, triceps, glutes, thighs, and calves	Chaturanga
UPWARD-FACING DOG	Arms, legs, and core	Urdhva mukha svanasana
DOWNWARD-FACING DOG	Hamstrings, calves, ankles, arches, hands, wrists, arms, shoulders, and abdominals	Adhomukha svanasana

PLAY DEAD Most yoga classes end in savasana, or corpse pose. The name is an apt one—you lie still and completely relaxed. It may look easy, but it takes practice to learn how to release the tension in all your muscles, yet still remain conscious and alert.

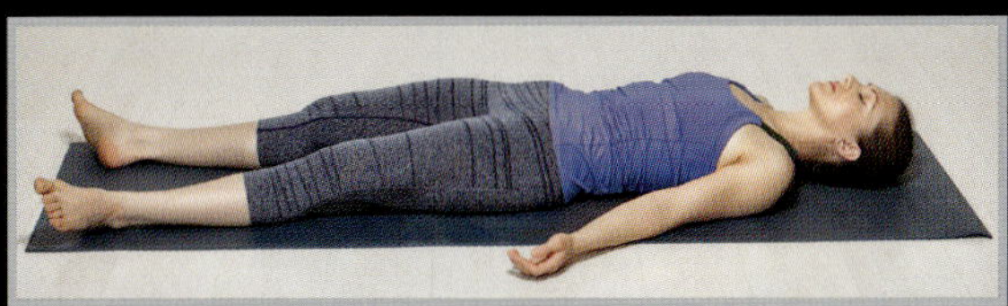

CONNECT MIND AND BODY WITH PILATES

Pilates aids the development of a balanced body by focusing on core strength, flexibility, body alignment, and stability, and by using your own body weight to create resistance. Joseph Pilates developed the system (originally called Contrology) in Germany in the early twentieth century. Inspired by his study of Asian philosophy and the Greek ideal of the perfect integrated human, he created a series of exercises based on the connection between the body and the mind. With its similarity to yoga and emphasis on resistance work, this versatile discipline exploded in popularity across the world in the 1980s—and has never lost its appeal.

Pilates, once the province of dancers and athletes, now benefits adults, seniors, and kids of all fitness levels, as well as those in rehab and women getting in shape after pregnancy. Advocates insist that Pilates not only makes them stronger, longer, and leaner, but also enables them to move with grace and coordination. They have better posture and feel more "aligned and together" as they handle the stress of their daily lives. The system can be practiced at any time and almost anywhere, and unlike fitness methods that require a lot of reps, Pilates asks only that, no matter how few you can perform, you should fully and precisely execute each movement.

PRACTICE THE PRINCIPLES

There are six principles of Pilates: concentration, centering, control, breathing, precision, and flow. When you integrate them during a workout, you can dramatically improve your fitness results.

CONCENTRATION Concentrate on the mind-body connection during an exercise, and picture the specific muscle pathways that will complete that movement. Then form a mental image of yourself performing the exercise correctly, in proper alignment.

CENTERING Pay special attention to the muscles of your core—the Pilates powerhouse—which include the abdomen, lower back, hips, and butt. They help all your body's muscles function more efficiently.

CONTROL Controlled exercises do not focus on intensity or reps, but on quality of movement. Control also develops strength, stamina, flexibility, equilibrium, and good posture—preventing stress on bones, muscles, and joints.

BREATHING Each Pilates exercise has a specific breathing pattern, so it takes practice in order to coordinate breathing and movement. Start by inhaling deeply through your nose during prep and return, and exhaling fully from your mouth during the rigorous phase.

PRECISION Pay attention to your form—in Pilates, quality matters more than quantity. Start and end correctly, tracing with your mind—and then your body—each step that composes the complete movement.

FLOW Exercise as though you were a dancer, with graceful connections and transitions from one position to the next as you lengthen your body.

GYM *etiquette*

TONE IT DOWN

The gym may not be a noise-free zone like a library, but it helps to keep the background noise down whenever possible, especially in classes like yoga and Pilates. It's best to keep your phone in the bag, but if you must have it, set it on vibrate while you exercise, so that incoming ringtones won't disturb others. If you must answer a call, go out to the lobby or parking lot. And try not to chat on the phone while using equipment that others are waiting for. You might appear more focused on your phone call than on your workout.

CHOOSE A PILATES CLASS

If your gym or studio has specialized Pilates equipment, take a few classes to familiarize yourself or, better yet, invest in some one-on-one time with a Pilates instructor who can help you apply the six principles. Exercising safely is a key aspect of this discipline, and you don't want to risk injury because you don't know how a certain apparatus works. Make sure to try out the reformer, a machine that utilizes pulleys and resistance from the participant's own body weight and with graduated levels of springs. Most of the Pilates exercises done on a mat can also be performed on the reformer.

EQUIP YOURSELF

Pilates exercises can be done on a mat on the floor or by using the special exercise apparatuses developed by Joseph Pilates. There are also portable Pilates aids you can use in class or at home.

MAT Pilates mats are thicker than yoga mats and not sticky. Look for a supportive mat at least a half-inch thick (1.27 cm) and long enough and wide enough so that you can exercise without shifting off the edges.

PILATES BALL This small inflatable ball, which measures about 9 inches (23 cm) in diameter, can be grasped between the knees to work those stubborn inner-thigh muscles or placed behind your back for support during mat exercises.

FOAM ROLLER These tubular aids comes in a variety of sizes, colors, and densities; they provide cushioning and can also be used for stretching, strengthening, balance training, and self-massage.

MAGIC CIRCLE Also called a fitness circle, exercise ring, or fitness ring, this flexible rubber-encased metal ring with two pliable handles adds gentle resistance to Pilates movements when you squeeze the sides together or place tension on it from the inside.

ADD TO YOUR FITNESS PLAN: PILATES STOMACH SERIES

FLATTEN YOUR TUMMY

Pilates is known for its ability to help you achieve a toned and flat midsection. The following workout, known as the Stomach Series, Abdominal Series, or Belly Burner, lets you sample five of the classical Pilates mat exercises that really challenge your abdominal endurance. Your ultimate goal is to move seamlessly from one exercise to the next. If you are new to Pilates, begin by working on the first exercise, then when you feel comfortable performing it with precision and control, move onto the next in the series, gradually adding until you can perform all five in one rhythmic flow.

A SINGLE LEG STRETCH Lie faceup on the mat. Exhale, and curl your head and shoulders up off the mat, bend both knees into your chest, extending one leg straight out. Put your outside hand on the ankle of your bent leg and your inside hand on the knee of your bent leg. Inhale, switching legs two times in one inhalation and switching hand placement simultaneously. Exhale, switching legs two times in one exhalation, keeping hands in their proper placement.

B DOUBLE LEG STRETCH Lie faceup on your mat, and then curl your upper body into a half-curl position, pulling your knees to your chest with your hands on your ankles. Inhale, simultaneously extending your arms back and your legs forward. Exhale while hugging your knees back into the center. Make sure you are keeping your upper body lifted off the mat.

C SCISSORS Lie faceup on your mat with your arms by your side and your legs raised in the tabletop position. Inhale, drawing in your abdominals. Exhale, reaching your legs straight up and lifting your head and shoulders off the mat. Inhale, holding the position while lengthening your legs. Exhale, stretch your right leg away from your body, and raise your left leg toward your trunk. Hold onto your left leg with both hands, pulsing twice with a small, rhythmic back-and-forth motion while keeping your shoulders down. Inhale, switching your legs in the air, and then exhale, reaching for the opposite leg.

D DOUBLE STRAIGHT LEG LOWER/LIFT Lie faceup on your mat, and extend both legs up to the ceiling, squeezing your heels, sitting bones, and inner thighs together as you externally rotate the legs in the Pilates V-stance. With hands behind the head and elbows wide, lengthen the back of your neck, and curl up into a C-curve with your shoulder blades cresting the mat. Inhale, and lower both of your legs. Exhale, as you draw your legs up using lower abs, not your hip flexors.

E CRISS CROSS Lie faceup on the mat with your legs in tabletop position. Place your hands behind your head with shoulders down and elbows wide. Exhale, and curl your upper body off the mat. Inhale, then exhale, and extend your right leg as you rotate your ribcage to the right, keeping your elbows wide as you bring your left armpit toward the right knee. Turn your torso a little more with a small pulse as you continue to exhale. Inhale, and return to center. Exhale, extend your left leg, and rotate your torso to the left. Continue to alternate sides.

EXERCISE	REPS	BENEFITS
SINGLE LEG STRETCH	4 to 12 reps with each leg	Strengthens abs, promotes coordination, and stabilizes torso
DOUBLE LEG STRETCH	4 to 6 reps	Strengthens and builds abdominal endurance, promotes coordination, and stabilizes trunk
SCISSORS	4 to 12 reps with each leg	Strengthens abs, stretches hamstrings and hip flexors, and increases spine flexibility
DOUBLE STRAIGHT LEG LOWER/LIFT	4 to 6 reps	Strengthens abs, lengthens legs, and strengthens hips flexors
CRISS CROSS	4 to 12 reps	Strengthens abs and obliques and challenges trunk rotation

KEEP GOOD FORM Form is all-important in Pilates, and certain positions will often come up during a mat workout.

NEUTRAL POSITION You maintain the natural curve of your spine—typically when lying on your back.

IMPRINTED POSITION Press your navel toward your spine. This move flattens your abdominal wall and lengthens and strengthens your lower-back muscles.

C-CURVE C-curve describes the shape of your back and spine when you scoop in your stomach, stretching the muscles surrounding your spine in the process.

PILATES V-STANCE The legs are together, straight, and rotated outward from the top of the thigh, which brings the heels together with toes pointing slightly out, forming a V.

TABLETOP You lie faceup with legs raised, knees bent, and shins parallel to the mat. From this position, you will then lift your torso for many Pilates exercises.

GO THROUGH THE MOTIONS

Each of your joints has a prescribed path that it follows, called its range of motion (ROM). In order for a joint to have full range of motion, it must have good flexibility, but as you age this flexibility is often compromised. Keeping your joints moving is therefore essential for maintaining easy movement. There are three kinds of exercises used to build, recover, and maintain ROM.

PASSIVE RANGE OF MOTION (PROM) Often used by older people with severe movement limitations or anyone recovering from a sports injury or joint replacement, PROM calls for you do nothing as a therapist or equipment (such as a knee machine) moves the compromised joint through the range of motion.

ACTIVE ASSISTIVE RANGE OF MOTION (AAROM) Here, you use the muscles surrounding a joint in order to perform the exercise, relying on help from a therapist, trainer, or equipment.

ACTIVE RANGE OF MOTION (AROM) With AROM exercises, you use the muscles surrounding a joint to do the movements with no outside assistance.

EXTEND YOUR RANGE

To keep your muscles and joints healthy, include a few ROM exercises in your fitness plan. The following sample exercises focus on ankles, knees, and shoulders—three areas at which you might notice compromised range of motion. Definitely target problem areas, but look for exercises that also target joints that are working well to maintain your body's full range of motion throughout your life.

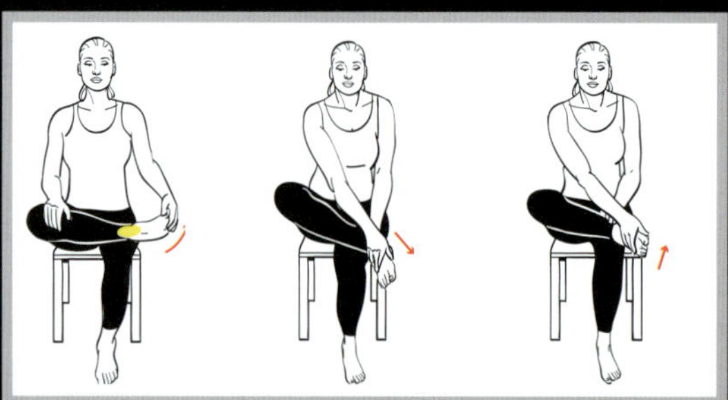

A ANKLE FLEX-EVERT-INVERT This exercise combines three moves to take your ankles through their full ROM.

HOW Sit with your right leg crossed over your left knee. Use your left hand to pull the top of your foot and toes toward you until you feel a gentle stretch on the top of your foot and ankle. Next, place your thumb on the top of your foot and your fingers across the bottom. Gently push your foot downward with a slight rotation so that your littlest toes rise slightly toward the ceiling. You should feel a gentle stretch on the inside of your ankle. Move your thumb to the bottom of your foot, and place your fingers across the top. Gently pull your foot so your smallest toe comes toward you, and your thumb pushes the inside of the ball of your foot away from you until you feel a gentle stretch on the outside of your ankle. Repeat all steps with your left foot.

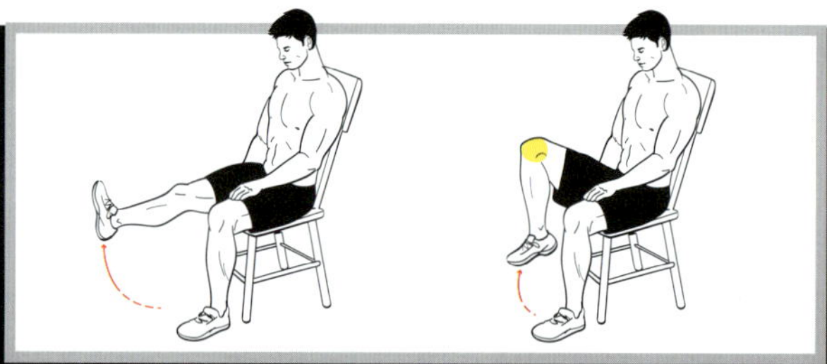

B EXTEND AND MARCH This compound move can improve the range of motion of your knees.

HOW Sit with your back straight and feet planted firmly on the floor. Extend one leg straight out, holding the extended position for 5 to 10 seconds. Slowly lower, and then bend the knee of the same leg to lift your leg as if you were marching. Slowly lower, and alternate extending and marching for the desired reps before switching to the other side.

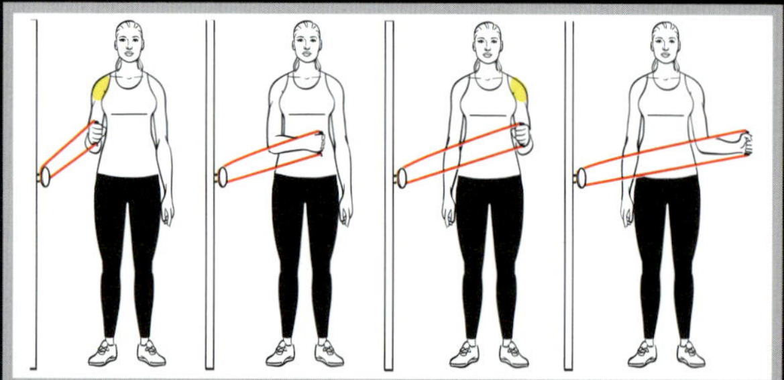

C INTERNAL AND EXTERNAL SHOULDER ROTATION This simple move targets your deltoids and rotator cuff to improve the range of motion of your shoulders.

HOW Attach a resistance band to a doorknob. Take hold of the handle, and, keeping your upper arm close to your side, bend your elbow to 90 degrees. Bring your hand across your body. Return to the start, switch hands, and bring your hand away from the middle of your body. Repeat in the opposite direction.

BOOK A FIT-CATION

If you are one of a growing number of individuals who now seek fitness-based destinations in lieu of relaxing vacation spots or family fun parks, here are some faraway locations that offer breathtaking scenery, along with lots of challenging physical activities. Be sure to check out a nearby Gold's Gym—they are part of the global community, after all—where you can put your travel pass to work.

PADDLE A BOARD Bohol in the Philippines, also known as God's Little Paradise, offers stand-up paddleboarding on the Loboc and Abatan Rivers, with miles of flat stretches for observing native wildlife, such as tarsiers, monitor lizards, and geckos. Paddleboarding provides a low-impact, full-body workout and improves balance. Also check out the multiple Gold's Gym locations in nearby Cebu City.

HIT THE SLOPES If the cardio exhilaration of skiing or snowboarding is your winter mania, try Japan's "powder paradise," Niseko. With nearly 50 feet of snow annually, Niseko's runs will definitely wow you. Try an afternoon of snowmobiling, and then have a soak in a volcanic hot spring. Tokyo, which you will pass through getting to and from Niseko, has a multitude of Gold's Gyms.

CHALLENGE THE ROCKIES The United States has no shortage of fitness destinations, but mountain biking in Ogden, Utah, also offers spectacular scenery and famous national parks, along with a full-muscle workout and lung-bursting cardio. Ogden attracts world-class riders, but provides trails for cyclists of every level. There are at least four Gold's Gyms in the Salt Lake City area.

FIND YOUR INNER LIGHT Follow in the footsteps of the Beatles, and travel to Rishikesh, India, to study in the yoga capital of the world. Seek enlightenment at the Ganga Aarti ceremony at Triveni Ghat or find peace while rafting on the holy Ganges River. The less spiritual can mingle with Bollywood stars at the Gold's Gym in Dehradum—or more than 90 other locations in India.

HIKE SIBERIA Every year, nearly 4,500 volunteers hack hundreds of miles of trails around stunning Lake Baikal, the deepest lake in the world, known as the Pearl of Siberia. This rugged wilderness offers hiking and outdoor activities, including seal sightings. Check out the Moscow Gold's Gyms before you embark on the Trans-Siberian Railway. All aboard for adventure!

EXPLORE MACHU PICCHU This ancient Inca city, one of the wonders of the New World, is located at an elevation of 8,000 feet (2,440 m)—so consider the cardio benefits of getting there during a four-day trek through three mountain passes. As you pass through Lima prior to embarking, check out one of the dozen Gold's Gyms in the area.

ASSESS YOUR PAIN

It's no surprise that professional athletes dread sports-related injuries that can take them out of the game. But many gym-goers also share this fear—they know that their success in the gym is based on regularity and repetition, and that anything that jeopardizes their schedule can derail their fitness goals. So if you are feeling any level of pain, you need to determine if your muscles are fatigued, sore, or actually injured—and whether or not to seek treatment. Here are some guidelines.

FATIGUE Muscles that are fatigued by strenuous work undergo physiological changes, including buildup of lactic acid (the "burn"), increased tissue acidity, and chemical energy depletion, so you might feel mild pain at the end of an exercise. This discomfort is temporary and diminishes quickly.

SORENESS Muscle pain that occurs a day or two after working out is known as delayed onset muscle soreness, or DOMS. It is associated with eccentric muscle contractions (the nonworking phase of lifting) and can be the result of microscopic tears in the muscle or connective tissue. DOMS may be mild, moderate, or so severe that sitting down in a chair is painful. Avoid any resistance training until it eases, usually in a day or two, and treat it with warm baths, heating pads, stretching, range-of-motion body movements, and acetaminophen.

INJURY Any pain that begins during or directly after working out and lasts for several days or more is likely to be a strain, also called a muscle pull. Strains happen when small tears occur in muscles and tendons after stretching them beyond capacity—a popping sensation is often the first sign. Strains can also occur from excessive training or a fall. They are classified as mild, moderate, or severe, but if you suspect a strain, have a doctor examine you as soon as possible in order to avoid complications.

REST AND RECOVER

It's great to have that "gung ho!" attitude when it comes to getting in shape, but it's also important to know when you need to say "gung whoa!" Recovery is the term that fitness trainers use when describing the time it takes sore muscles to repair themselves. Ideally, you should wait for at least 48 hours before focusing on the same muscle group, so stagger your target areas—upper body followed by lower body, for example. As well as helping you physically recuperate, a period of rest also allows you to recover psychologically.

Ask the EXPERT

STRAIN OR SPRAIN?

This is a question that fitness trainers often hear, and there is a distinct difference. Strains and sprains both involve damage to the body's supporting framework: the bones, muscles, tendons, and ligaments.

When a muscle or tendon—a fibrous cord connecting muscles to bones—is stretched or torn, the injury is called a strain. Acute strains occur at the junction where the muscle is becoming a tendon, when the muscle is stretched and suddenly contracts, as during running or jumping. Chronic strains develop from overuse or repetitive stress, such as serving a tennis ball, which leads to an inflamed tendon—tendonitis. Strains can be accompanied by symptoms including sharp pain, swelling, bruising, or redness. They are treated by rest, cold packs, compression, and elevation.

Ligaments are the tissues that connect bones to each other. Sprains involve the stretching or tearing of a ligament or a joint capsule. Forcing a joint beyond its normal range of motion, such rolling your ankle, is the most common cause of sprains. You will experience pain and inflammation, and, because ligaments provide joint stability, you may temporarily lose the ability to move your limb properly.

Both strains and sprain require speedy medical intervention, but with due care, most of these injuries heal without long-term problems.

ICE IT OR APPLY HEAT

There are two accepted ways to ease muscle pain or injury (icing and heating) but most people have no clue which treatment to apply, and so they end up using the wrong one, or both . . . or neither. Here are some guidelines to make remembering less difficult.

ICING The application of cold packs (or bags of frozen peas) to an injury relieves pain by numbing the area as well as reducing swelling, inflammation, and bleeding. Always ice the site immediately (remember: Ice Immediately) after the injury occurs and for the next two days. To make your own cold pack, freeze a wet, folded hand towel inside a plastic zip bag.

HEATING Applying a heating pad, warm compress, or other source of heat brings blood to an injured area and reduces joint stiffness and muscle spasms. Use these methods only after 48 hours of icing an injury. And don't apply a heating pad directly to the skin—wrap it in flannel or a towel.

CALL THE DOCTOR!

If you are experiencing pain and suspect you have a strain, sprain, or other exercise-related injury—meaning the pain began while you were exercising and did not let up for a day or two—it's time to visit a health care professional to get an examination. After determining the type and severity of the injury, he or she will recommend a protocol to expedite healing, possibly including physical therapy. In the case of some more extreme strains, such as a ripped tendon, surgery might be in order. But even with more moderate injuries, proper and timely treatment is imperative—otherwise scar tissue could form around the tear and limit your range of motion, requiring visits to a physiotherapist or chiropractor.

In addition to strains and sprains, here are some injuries that might require a doctor's care.

BACKACHE Even though strength and flexibility exercises often ultimately relieve lower-back pain, you might initially experience lumbar aches when you begin to work out or perform repetitive motions. Make sure that you warm up properly, and treat any pain with stretching, strength work, and cold packs.

GROIN PULL Stressing groin muscles that are stiff, a bit weak, and prone to strains is frequently the cause of this painful condition. Always go slowly when exploring the range of motion of a new exercise. Treat by icing the inner thigh and with compression, ibuprofen, and stretching and strengthening exercises. Full recovery could take 12 weeks.

SHIN SPLINTS Those stabbing pains along the front of the lower legs are caused by intensifying your running or biking routine too quickly or not allowing enough recovery time. Shin splints occur from damage to one of two muscle groups along the shinbone. Treatment includes cessation of activity, stretching, strength work, cold packs, and ibuprofen, and adding arch supports or heel lift inserts to running shoes.

RUNNER'S KNEE The knee may be the most likely body part to be injured during exercise. Runner's knee, which can be caused by tight hamstrings, improper foot support, or weak thigh muscles, causes a dull pain around the front of the knee (patella) where it connects with bottom of the thighbone (femur). It is especially painful going up and down stairs. Treatment involves cessation of running, cold packs, compression, elevation, ibuprofen, stretching, and the addition of arch supports.

BLISTERS These tender fluid-filled bubbles can ruin a workout or run; if they become infected, they take a lot longer to heal and can adversely affect your routine. To reduce the friction that causes blisters, wear properly fitting shoes and moisture-wicking socks. A bit of petroleum jelly also helps lubricate blister-prone areas.

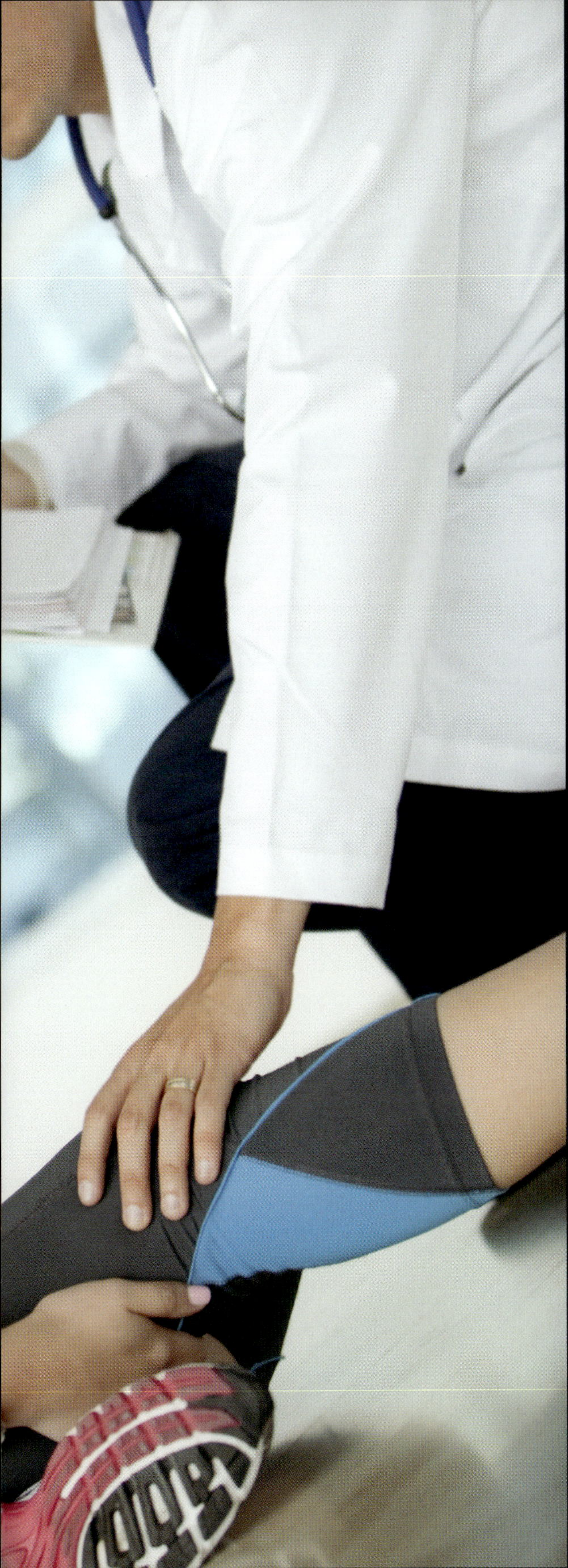

TAKE IT EASY

If you are diagnosed with a serious sports or fitness-related injury, it's important that you abide by your doctor's instructions regarding recuperation time. Muscles, tendons, and ligaments can sometimes take longer than bones to mend. Make sure that you don't skip or shorten any physical therapy sessions, and if home exercises are called for, do them for as long as prescribed.

Another part of recovery is understanding what happened to cause the injury and doing your best to ensure that it will not occur again. If you forgot warming up, overtrained, or tried a difficult move without guidance from a trainer, then those are situations you can avoid in future. If you took a misstep, got a cramp, or fell, then those are not circumstances you could have changed. Accepting that and moving on is important. Even the best and strongest athletes occasionally suffer a hard knock through no fault of their own.

COME BACK SLOWLY

Once your doctor or physical therapist clears you to go back to the gym, make sure to follow these suggestions for a seamless—and painless—re-entry.

MAKE A PLAN Work with your doctor, physiotherapist, and trainer to come up with an exercise-based rehab plan. Your physical therapist or trainer can also spot any faulty movements or muscle imbalances that might cause future injuries.

STAY FUELED During recovery and re-entry you need to eat right and maintain proper hydration. Avoid alcohol, refined sugar, or white flour; stick with lean protein, complex carbs, and lots of greens. You might also consider taking joint-building supplements like glutamine or MSM and chondroitin.

TAKE YOUR TIME Even after you start to feel like your old, pre-injury self, stick with your rehab plan for at least another two weeks. That way you continue to build strength. Once your rehab rules have relaxed, continue to focus on exercises that emphasize stability, flexibility and the core.

ROLL WITH IT It's critical to warm up your injured muscles before exercising, so consider massaging the vulnerable spots with a foam roller.

MAINTAIN YOUR MOJO

Even if you are seeing results, it can be hard to stay motivated at the gym week in and week out. You might also hit a slump and find you're making excuses to stay home. Gold's Gym (and the Mayo Clinic) offer some possible solutions that will raise your level of enthusiasm and beat the blahs.

SET SHORT-RANGE GOALS We're always told to look at the big picture, but sometimes dealing with things in smaller increments is a lot easier on our psyches. Break your fitness goals into doable segments—for instance focus on losing 2 pounds a week rather than 24 pounds in 12 weeks. And be sure to write down those goals.

KEEP IT FUN Who said working out had to be so serious? Break up your strength or cardio routines with some free-form dancing to your MP3 player or do a circuit around the track—while skipping.

MAKE A SWITCH It helps to vary your workouts. If you always head to the treadmill for cardio, give the elliptical a go. Try a new piece of equipment, such as an EZ bar or a new modality, such as TRX or battle rope training, or sign up for a lively class, like Zumba or PiYo. Trying something new helps keep boredom at bay.

FIND OTHER OUTLETS Make fitness part of your home life, not just a gym experience. Get off the couch, and get yourself moving. Weed the garden, mow the lawn, paint the guest room, rake the leaves, hand polish the stair rails, or de-clutter the closets—remember, if you're moving, your core's moving.

DON'T BE RIGID If you make yourself a hostage to your fitness goals, then the gym will start to feel like a prison. Take a day or two off if you need to chill. Forcing yourself to exercise can sour you and end up derailing your efforts a lot quicker than a few days of R&R.

GIVE YOURSELF A REWARD If you've met a tough goal or beaten a personal best, how about rewarding yourself with something special? You can upgrade your gear—such as buying yourself new running shoes or a tote-bag for your yoga mat—or you could treat yourself to a new activity—such as a fun dance class or yoga in the park.

MAKE FITNESS TIME FAMILY AND FRIEND TIME Maybe this message keeps getting repeated because it's true—it is always more entertaining to work out with a friend or loved one. Make gym time couple time or try organizing an informal game of soccer or street hockey with your kids or friends.

BRING ON THE SANDMAN

Adequate sleep is a key part of fitness—it is when the body and brain replenish. Lack of sleep won't just leave you foggy; chronic insomnia can also make you prone to diabetes, depression, cardiovascular disease, and weight gain. Still, you'd think that getting regular exercise would send you straight to dreamland at night, but even certain pro athletes find that sleep eludes them, resulting in a loss of aerobic endurance. Below are some triggers for sleep problems, along with how to avoid them so that you can wake up feeling fresh and alert.

KICK THE CAFFEINE Most people know enough not to drink caffeine in the evening, but even a cup of tea at 4:00 p.m. can affect your sleep patterns. If you are a restless sleeper, boycott any drinks with caffeine after 2:00 p.m.

SNOOZE WITH SEROTONIN Heavy meals should be avoided before bedtime, but some foods can actually help you sleep. An all-carbohydrate snack is beneficial for getting your body to make the most of its own store of sleep-inducing serotonin (as well as tryptophan, an amino acid that is converted to serotonin in the body). Try a late-night snack of graham crackers, or you can add serotonin or serotonin-precursor supplements, such as 5-HTP, to your nutrition plan.

SAY NO TO NIGHTCAPS It's true that alcohol will make you sleepy, but it is also true that it can disturb the second half of your sleep cycle and decrease deep sleep.

BATHE EARLY One traditional cure for insomnia—taking a hot bath before heading to bed—may actually keep you up. Anything that raises your body temperature near bedtime can stop you from falling asleep. The body likes to be cool as it slumbers, which is why we often wake up to find one foot outside the covers.

RELAX WITH YOGA Shedding mental and physical stress is an ideal way to invite sleep. At bedtime, try some gentle yoga moves, such as the reclined butterfly. Lie supine with your soles together, knees drooping. Then close your eyes, and inhale through your nose while slowly counting to four; exhale counting backwards to one. A 10-minute session should ease you into sleep.

BANISH LIGHT Exposure to bright lights or computer screens—which signal daytime to our brains—before bedtime can delay the onset of sleep. Dim the lights as you get ready for bed, and then turn off all technology, including your cell phone text alert.

PAT YOURSELF ON THE BACK

At some point in your fitness journey, you will realize that you got out of bed in the morning without any creakiness or pain. Perhaps you *ran* to the car in the rain. Or you slipped into that party dress and it actually fit. "Wow," you think with a bit of shock. "It's really working."

This is where you congratulate yourself, when you comprehend that through dedication, application, and hard work, you have changed your physical appearance for the better. And that there are so many beneficial changes on the inside, ones you can't even see—like increased strength, greater stamina, a healthier heart and lungs, a boosted metabolism, and improved flexibility. Like being at a lower risk for high blood pressure and type 2 diabetes. Or that feeling you can conquer the world. So tell yourself "Well done!"—and eat a celebratory cupcake or plate of French fries. And then get right back on the gym floor, and start to work your butt off. *Again.*

KEEP UP THE GREAT WORK

For some people, reaching their goal is not the most difficult part of a fitness plan. Maybe you're one of them. You can apply yourself like gangbusters initially, but can't sustain the momentum to hold onto those gains afterward. If so, here are some suggestions to stop you from relapsing and losing the precious inroads you've made toward better health and fitness.

UPDATE YOUR GOALS Maintenance will require a different mindset than conditioning. Change your focus by giving yourself fitness goals outside the gym—joining a charity race, for example, or starting up a hiking group. Also engage in a physical activity you enjoy for its own sake, like horseback riding or softball.

SIDESTEP YOUR TRIGGERS Don't let personal drama or any negative emotions impact your health decisions during transition. If something is so upsetting that you vow to ditch the gym for the next month, take a yoga class instead to regain your centered self.

PASS IT ALONG Rather than spending your time obsessively recording miles or calories, become a message-bearer to keep yourself accountable. Share knowledge and experience with your friends or family members, and encourage them to find their own path to wellness.

BE PATIENT Remind yourself frequently that it takes time to shift gears into maintenance mode. For instance, ease up on high-intensity workouts and lower your caloric demand accordingly, but don't stop scheduling those gym visits or trainer sessions—and never lose that healthy desire to improve yourself. Remember that fitness is a lifelong journey, not a destination.

COACH
TRAIN FOR LIFE

GLOSSARY

aerobic Relating to activity that increases the body's demand for oxygen thereby resulting in temporary increase in breathing and heart rate.

alignment The proper positioning or state of adjustment of parts in relation to each other.

bodybuilder A person who develops their physique through diet and exercise for competitions.

chronic Continuing or occurring again and again for a long time.

diaphragm The partition separating the chest and abdominal cavities in mammals.

discipline Control gained by enforcing obedience or order.

endurance The ability to sustain a prolonged stressful effort or activity.

technique The manner in which basic physical movements are used.

massage The manipulation of tissues by rubbing, kneading, or tapping, with the hand or an instrument.

meditation To engage in mental exercise for the purpose of reaching a heightened level of awareness.

motivation The inspiration or drive to complete an action.

passive Without active response or resistance.

physical therapist A person who treats a disease or injury by physical methods and exercise.

physique The form, size, and development of a person's body.

pliable Easily bent or flexible.

recuperate To recover health or strength.

regimen A systematic plan to improve and maintain health.

resistance The power or capacity to resist, or push away.

stimuli Something that rouses or incites to activity.

torso The upper part of a human body.

FURTHER READING

BOOKS

Ellsworth, Abigail. *Anatomy of Yoga: An Instructor's Inside Guide to Improving Your Poses.* Richmond Hill, ON: Firefly Books, Limited, 2013.

James, Sara. *Yoga & Pilates* (Integrated Life for Fitness). Broomall, PA: Mason Crest, 2015.

Kaminoff, Leslie, and Amy Matthews. *Yoga Anatomy-2nd Edition.* Champaign, IL: Human Kinetics Publishers, 2011.

Oren, Goldie Karpel. *Yoga Fitness* (Fitness for the Mind and Body). New York, NY: Rosen Publishing, 2015.

Ungaro, Alycea. *Pilates Body in Motion.* London, UK: DK, 2002.

WEBSITES

All About Pilates
https://www.pilates.com/BBAPP/V/pilates/index.html
Research the origins of pilates and try out suggested practices.

The Science of Yoga
https://yogainternational.com/article/view/scientific-research-how-yoga-works
Discover the science behind yoga and why it works.

Yoga History
http://www.yogabasics.com/learn/history-of-yoga/
Explore yoga's evolution through history.

INDEX

R

S

T

U

V

Y